CONTENTS
OF
VOLUME III

THE
BOOK OF TRADES
OR
LIBRARY
OF
USEFUL ARTS

VOLUME III

1818

Edited by Beryl Hurley

Published by Wiltshire Family History Society

Originally printed in
The Book of English Trades and Library of the Useful Arts
London:
Stereotyped by G. SIDNEY, Northumberland-street,
for Richard Phillips;
Published by J. Souter, at the Juvenile Library
73, St. Paul's Church-Yard.

July 27th, 1818

The fourteen trades in this Volume are taken from a later edition of The Book of Trades than those published by Wiltshire Family History Society in Volumes I & II. This later edition was published in 1818 and contains most of the trades from the three volumes published in 1811, with the addition of the trades in this volume.

Wiltshire Family History Society

Registered Charity No. 290284

ISBN No. 1 898714 02 9

1994

Our thanks to Michael Field, of Binbrook, Lincs, for the loan of an original copy of the 1818 edition, enabling us to reproduce these trades.

THE ATTORNEY

AN ATTORNEY primarily signifies any one who is appointed by another to transact any business for him in his absence: but an *Attorney-at-Law*, of whom we are now to speak, is a person who manages the *Law* business of another, for whom he is retained; the term being analogous to the procurator or proctor of the civilians and canonists in the ecclesiastical courts.

Anciently, according to the old Gothic constitutions, every suitor was obliged to appear and prosecute or defend his suit in person, unless by special license from the king; and this still continues to be the rule in criminal cases. But by sundry old statutes from that of Westm. 2. c. 10, permission was granted to attornies to prosecute or defend any civil suit in the absence of the parties. An idiot, however, cannot at this day, prosecute or defend by his Attorney, but must appear in person.

Attornies are admitted to the execution of their office, by the superior courts at Westminster Hall. They are considered as officers of the respective courts in which they are admitted; on which account, they enjoy many privileges; and are peculiarly subject to the censure and animadversion of the judges. In order to enable a person to practise as an Attorney, in any of these courts, he must be admitted and sworn an Attorney of that particular court: and an Attorney in the court of King's Bench cannot practise in the Common-Pleas, nor can an attorney in the Common-Pleas, practise in the Court of King's Bench. To practise in the court of Chancery, it is also necessary to be admitted a Solicitor therein.

The business of an Attorney is one of the most important occupations which can engage the attention of the conscientious man, in the present state of society. To him, the oppressed repair to learn by what means the oppressor is to be resisted; to him, the orphan and the friendless look, as to one who knows how to direct them to recover their property or their rights. The Attorney it is to whom, as a *Conveyancer* in preparing deeds, bonds, mortgages, marriage settlements, &c. we confide the transfer and security of our monies, our goods, and our estates. It is the Attorney before whom we lay those documents, upon his opinion of which we buy and sell land, houses, and a variety of other property depending more especially upon what is usually called, the *Title* to their possession. By these means, it is the Attorney who has an opportunity of knowing the most intimate affairs of individuals in every relative situation in life; and it is the Attorney, thus invested with so much power, who has an opportunity of becoming either a blessing or a curse to the neighbourhood in which he resides: for such is now the complexity of our laws, that it is scarcely possible for a plain and simple-minded man to meddle with them without having his Attorney at his elbow, unless he choose to run the great risk of being overthrown and defeated, even in the best of causes.

If, therefore, instead of that manliness and integrity, which should dignify an Attorney, he abuse the confidence reposed in him, and descend to the low and petty arts of fomenting litigation and strife between contending parties, for the mere purpose of filling his own pocket, or to gratify the malignity of some tyrant of power, it is evident that there is no term in language sufficiently strong to designate the man. If, on the contrary, an upright man, well acquainted with the laws and their forms, but knowing the fallibility of human nature, and the fallible nature of testimony too, if such a man should be an Attorney, how much strife can he not prevent, how much misery and distress can he not cure!

The legislature has, from time to time, passed various acts relative to the conduct and powers of Attornies, who are liable to be punished in a summary way, either by attachment, or having their names struck off the roll, for ill practice, attended with fraud and corruption, and committed against the obvious rules of justice and common honesty; but the court will not easily be prevailed on to proceed in this manner, if it appears that the matter complained of was rather owing to neglect or accident, than design; or if the party injured, has other remedy by act of Parliament, or action at law.

Attornies have the privilege to sue, and be sued, only in the courts at Westminster, where they practise.

Besides the obligations of fidelity to his client the Attorney owes him secresy: and in certain cases, an action lies at the suit of his client for neglect of duty: but such actions are extremely rare.

Persons who are bound clerks to Attornies or Solicitors, are to cause affidavits to be made and filed of the execution of the articles, names and places of abode, of attorney or solicitor, and clerk, and none are to be admitted till the affidavit be produced and read in court: no attorney having discontinued business, is to take a clerk. Clerks are to serve actually during the whole time, and make affidavits thereof. Persons admitted sworn clerks in Chancery, or serving a clerkship to such, may be admitted *Solicitor*. By the stat. 23 Geo. 2. c. 26, any person duly admitted a Solicitor, may be admitted an Attorney, without any fee for the oath, or any stamp to be impressed on the parchment wherin his admission shall be written, in the same manner as, by stat. Geo. 2. c. 23.| 20, Attornies may be admitted Solicitors.

Every Attorney and Solicitor must annually take out a certificate from the courts in which they practise: if the attorney resides in London, and has been admitted three years or upwards, the stamp duty, for his certificate, is ten pounds: if less than three years, five pounds, if he reside *elsewhere*, and has been admitted three years or more, the stamp for his certificate is six pounds; less than three years, three pounds.

The stamp duty for the articles for an Attorney's clerk, in order to have admission to the courts of law, is one hundred and ten pounds.

The late acts of parliament having made it more expensive to become an attorney, it is presumed that incompetent, vulgar, and illiterate persons must have more difficulty to get into the profession, and in consequence, the respectability of the attorney ought to be increased.

The expense of establishing a young man as an Attorney, consists in an apprentice fee of sometimes three, or even five hundred guineas, the expense afterwards, in admission to the courts of law, the stamp duties and books; which, if properly selected, amount in value, to many hundred pounds. Some young men who are desirous of excelling as Attornies, will, after the expiration of their clerkship, place themselves in the office of some eminent Attorney in London, to obtain experience, or become pupils to a Barrister for a limited time.

THE BLEACHER

BLEACHING is the art by which those manufactures, which have vegetable substances for their raw material, are freed from the colouring matter with which such substances are naturally combined, or accidentally stained; and the pure vegetable fibre, deprived of these coloured matters, is left to reflect the different rays of light in due proportion, so as to appear white.

Besides the spoils of animals, mankind, to supply their natural want of covering, have, in all countries, had recourse to vegetable substances, preferring those whose fibres excelled in strength, durability, and pliancy; and experience having proved, that flax and cotton were well adapted to such purposes, these substances have been very generally adopted, and formed into such cloths as the skill and industry of the weavers could execute.

It would soon be observed, that the action of water, together with that of the sun and air, rendered those rude cloths whiter than they were at their first formation; and since the first step towards refinement is to add beauty to utility, as the state of society improved, a desire to give them a pure and spotless white would naturally arise. The idea of white raiment being the emblem of innocence and peace, which seems to have been very early entertained, would make every means for facilitating the removal of natural or adventitious stains more earnestly studied.

Accident would probably discover, that a certain degree of putrid fermentation carried off colouring matter from vegetable fibres. Hence the practice of macerating cloth in water, mixed with putrid urine and the dung of domestic animals, which has been continued to our days.

From the earliest accounts we have of India, Egypt, and Syria, it appears that these enlightened nations knew the efficacy of natron, (the nitre of scripture), an impure mineral alkali, found in these countries, for combining with, and carrying off, the colouring matters with which cloth is stained; and it is still found in great abundance by the present inhabitants, and used for the same purpose. We are, also, informed by Pliny, that the ancient Gauls were acquainted with the use of a lixivium, extracted from the ashes of burnt vegetables, as a detergent, and knew how to combine this lixivium with animal oil to form soap.

But though these nations appear to have early acquired some knowledge of the art of bleaching, the progress of improvement which they made in it, when compared to the advantages which some of them enjoyed, was very inconsiderable. The same practices seem to have been handed down from one generation to another, without any material improvement. In India it would appear, that the art of bleaching, as well as that of staining of cloths of various colours, are not in greater perfection at present, than they are described to have been in the days of Herodotus. Even in Europe, when the arts, after they have been once introduced, have generally made rapid progress, the art of bleaching made very slow advances, till towards the end of the eighteenth century.

At this period the oxymuriatic acid, and its effects, were discovered by Scheele; and its applications to the art of bleaching, by Berthollet, has given it an impulse towards perfection unknown in the history of any other art. It now became evident that oxygen had an affinity with the colouring matters with which cotton and linen manufactures are stained; and that, by a proper use of the alkalis, along with the oxymuriatic acid, these colouring matters could be removed, and the goods rendered white, in a space of time almost instantaneous, when compared with the former method of bleaching.

Upon these discoveries the present improved state of bleaching is founded. The machinery and utensils used in bleaching are various, according to the business done by the bleacher. Where linen or heavy cotton cloths are whitened, and the business is carried on to a considerable extent, the machinery is both complicated and expensive. It consist chiefly of a water-wheel, sufficiently powerful for giving motion to the wash-stocks, dash-wheels, squeezers, &c. with any other operations where power is required.

After the process of washing by the dash-wheel, the water is compressed from the cloth by means of squeezers. The boilers used in bleaching, are of the common form, having a stop-cock at bottom for running off the waste ley. They are commonly made of cast iron, and are capable of containing from three hundred to six hundred gallons of water, according to the extent of the business done.

The substances used in bleaching, are chiefly pot and pearl ashes, soda, soap, oxymuriate of potash, oxymuriate of lime, manganese, muriatic acid, and sulphuric acid.

The common operations of bleaching, consist of steeping, bucking, boiling, immersion in the oxymuriatic acid, souring, washing, &c.

Steeping, is a process made use of for cleaning the cloths designed to be bleached, from the substances used by the weavers in their manufacture, and is principally effected by means of an alkaline ley at a blood-heat.

Bucking is one of the most important operations in the bleaching of linen goods: it consists in boiling the cloths in caustic alkaline ley, by a heat gradually raised, and thereby dissolving, and taking off their colouring matter.

Boiling, in the bleaching of linen cloth, is only used when the goods are nearly white with pearl ashes alone, or with pearl ashes along with soap, towards the end of the whitening process.

Immersion in the oxymuriate of potash. The linens, after being clean washed, are steeped in it for twelve hours, then drained, and washed for being further bucked or boiled.

Souring is, in general, the last or finishing process in bleaching, as afterwards the linens are only further washed in spring water, in order to their being blued and made up for the market.

In preparing the sour, into a large fir tub, lined with lead, as much sulphuric acid is added to water as will give it the acidity of strong vinegar. The acid and water must be well mixed together before immersing the linens, which are generally steeped in it for twelve hours.

Where washing is mentioned, it must be always understood that the linen is taken to the wash-stocks, or dash-wheel, and washed well in them for some hours. This part of the work can never be overdone; and on its being properly executed, between every part of the bucking, boiling, steeping in the oxymuriatic acid, and souring, not a little of the success of bleaching depends. By exposure, is meant that the linen cloth is taken and spread upon the bleach-green, for four, six, or eight days, according as the routine of business calls for the return of the cloth, in order to undergo further operations.

There are a variety of processes adopted for the bleaching of goods of different degrees of fineness: muslin, for instance, requiring a process varied from that adopted for coarse linen; and more delicacy is still necessary in bleaching coloured cottons and pulicates into which permanent colours are woven.

The plate represents the bleaching of cloth, as it is now sometimes practised, by pouring water upon it, as it lies exposed in the bleaching-ground, to whiten, by the united operations of the sun, the air, and moisture, the cloths having previously passed through propert alkaline leys: this is called the *old* method of bleaching, the *new* is by the more expeditious process of oxymuriatic acid, &c.

THE BOOKSELLER

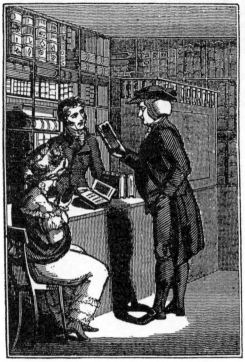

Before the invention of printing, and of the manufacture of paper from linen, books were so scarce and dear, as to be without the reach of all but persons of considerable opulence. Though the materials of which they were made had been as cheap and as plentiful as paper is at present, the labour of multiplying copies in manuscript, would always have kept their numbers comparatively scanty, and their price high.

Hence in all the nations of antiquity, learning was almost exclusively confined to the people of rank, and the lower orders were only rescued from total ignorance, by the reflected light of their superiors, and raised above the rudeness of barbarism, by that partial improvement which men of cultivation and refinement necessarily impart, in a greater or less degree, to all within the sphere of their influence. The Papyrus, a kind of broad-leaved rush, being the cheapest material for the reception of writing, was of course in most general use.

When this could no longer be procured, in consequence of the conquest of Egypt by the Saracens, *parchment* was then substituted, but it was so difficult to be procured, that it was customary to erase the writing of an ancient manuscript to make room for some other composition. In this manner many of the best works of antiquity were lost for ever. Books were for many ages so scarce, that to present a book to a religious house, was thought so valuable a donation as to merit eternal salvation, and it was offered on the altar with great ceremony.

The making of paper, such as we now see it, is dated by the generality of writers at the eleventh or twelfth century; but the honour of the discovery is claimed by different and distant nations. The first book which was printed on paper manufactured in England, came out without a date about 1495 or 1496, about fifty years after the invention of printing, although for a long while afterwards it was principally brought from abroad.

The art of printing necessarily produced the Bookseller. Indeed, we believe that the earlier printers were also Booksellers, as are some of the Printers of the present day; but the lapse of years, and a variety of other circumstances, have generated many trades and subdivisions of trades, to our forefathers wholly unknown. Even the trade of a Bookseller is considerably subdivided, at least in London.

The Bookseller of the present day is a person of considerable importance in the republic of letters, more especially if he combines those particular branches of the trade denominated *Proprietor* and *Publisher*: for it is to such men our men of genius take their productions for sale: and the success of works of genius very frequently depends upon their spirit, probity, and patronage. It is also to such men that the reading public generally are indebted for almost every important work of a voluminous kind. Those bulky and valuable volumes, the various Encyclopaedias, would never have made their appearance had not a Bookseller, or a combination of Booksellers, entered upon the speculation by employing men of science and learning in the various departments of those works, and embarking large capitals in the undertaking. The sums of money employed in such concerns as these are immense, and the regularity and dispatch with which some of these extensive bookselling concerns are conducted, exceed the conception of those persons wholly unacquainted with the affair.

Paternoster Row has been, for a long period, notorious as the place in which some of these large establishments are carried on, and where a great number of Booksellers' shops and ware-houses abound. The Stationers' Company have a Hall not far distant from it, where a copy of every book must, by a late Act of Parliament, be deposited when published in order to secure to the proprietor or author of it the sole profits arising from its publication and sale. A copy must also be deposited in the British Museum, the two Universities, and some other public establishments, amounting to eleven in number.

In London, and some other large bookselling establishments in the kingdom, books in the wholesale way are sold in quires: lists of such sales are constantly handed about amongst the large dealers in books.

Some Booksellers in London confine their trade to particular departments. There are Law Booksellers, Medical Booksellers, Foreign Booksellers, Religious booksellers, Booksellers of Education and Children's books; others deal in old books only, and some principally in rare and scarce books: the rarity being in numerous instances the criterion of value. A rare copy of the *Decameron* of Boccacio was sold a few years ago, for upwards of *two thousand pounds*, when the book might have been bought in London at the same time, recently printed, for a few shillings! The form of a book, the style of the printing, and the name of the printer, add materially to the value of these conceits. The books called black-letter books are also much esteemed.

The sale of some books of fancy and genius, in the present age, if not in price, has exceeded in number the books of any former period. We may mention those of Lord Byron, Mr. Walter Scott, and Mr. Thomas Moore, as instances of the extraordinary and rare good fortune of these gentlemen. Whilst other works, perhaps of equal, although of course of very different merit, have sunk almost dead-born from the press.

The sale of periodical publications is in Great Britain of considerable importance: it consists of Magazines, Reviews, and a variety of other productions published for the most part monthly. Other works are frequently divided into numbers and published weekly in order to make the price, when they are bulky, come easy to the purchaser. By these means an infinity of books, and a vast body of information, have been diffused throughout the community, and which have made the trade of a Bookseller one of the greatest interest and importance to mankind.

It is by the diffusion of knowledge by books that all species of tyranny and oppression can be most effectually resisted; it is by the diffusion of books, that mankind become acquainted with their moral and religious duties; and it is also by books that men generally become distinguished for their intelligence, probity, and worth; for where the diffusion of knowledge by books has not taken place, there we most commonly find the relative and social duties at a very low ebb.

Newspapers are another species of books very valuable in their kind; but as they are not often sold by Booksellers, we content ourselves with merely making mention of them.

The plate represents the inside of a retail Bookseller's shop. No explanation whatever can be necessary.

THE CHEMIST & DRUGGIST

CHEMISTRY is the science which treats of those events or changes in natural bodies, by which new bodies are composed, or compound ones divided: its principal object is, to ascertain the principles or elements of which bodies are composed, and the laws by which the simple atoms of matter unite together, and form compounds.

Neither the origin, or primitive meaning of the word Chemistry, is accurately known. That it was used by the Greeks, soon after the commencement of the Christian aera, is certain, and many reasons coincide to render it probable, that it was of Egyptian origin. It is certain that the Chemistry of the ancients was the name of an art of some kind or another. Suidas, a Greek writer, mentions this particularly in his Lexicon.

The honour of laying the foundation of the present science of Chemistry, belongs to John Joachim Becher, who was born at Spires, in Germany, in 1645, where he became professor of medicine, and afterwards was appointed first physician to the elector of Mentz and Bavaria; but he ended his days in England. His writings testify with what success he applied himself to the study of this important branch of natural philosophy. To name the illustrious men who laboured in this science, during the eighteenth century, would require a volume. Priestly, Scheele, Macquer, Black, Cavendish, and Lavoisier, are amongst the most eminent, some of whom have only, within a few years past, paid the debt of nature. Of living Chemists, Sir Humphry Davy, and Mr. Brande, the present professor of Chemistry at the Royal Institution are eminently conspicuous.

Formerly the preparations of drugs were divided into two classes, termed *chemical* and *galenical*; idle distinctions, which have nearly disappeared before the light which modern Chemistry has spread abroad. A more correct and just classification has obtained both in the science itself, and in the terms and names of the several substances, in consequence of the assiduity with which chemical investigation has been followed in many of the nations of Europe. The hidden qualities, or supposed qualities of matter, are now no longer taken for granted; all must be weighed in the balance of experiment, and submitted to the severe test of philosophical truth: it is utterly impossible to say where our experiments may end. *Water*, for a long time, supposed to be a simple body, is now known to be a compound one; the great powers which have been latterly acquired by a modified operation of electricity, called the *Galvanic* apparatus, have unfolded to us results and changes as extraordinary as unexpected, and which lead us not less to wonder at the infinite variety of the powers abounding in nature, than at the ingenuity and perseverance of man; we may well conclude, therefore, that much yet remains to be explored: a deep mine for the future active genius of research.

It is scarcely possible to name a thing in the natural world, to which Chemistry does not either directly, or indirectly, apply. Heat, light, air, electricity, the phenomena of the seasons, the different climates, the sea, mountains, volcanoes, mines, have all an intimate connexion with this the first of all sciences. The boiling of a potato, the roasting of a piece of beef, the baking of a pie, or of a loaf of bread, are equally objects of the science of Chemistry. But, in a more confined sense, the Chemist is employed in the composition and decomposition of medicines designed for the cure or alleviation of disease: and in the manufacture of a variety of articles used in the arts.

The Chemist of trade, might be defined the maker of medicines; the Druggist, the seller of them. In London, and many other places, a Chemist and Druggist are frequently combined in the same person, and in other instances, the trade of a Chemist is divided into a variety of branches. Some prepare compositions of mercury; others refine saltpetre; some distil essential oils; and others, as the Apothecaries' Company, prepare the greatest part of the compositions themselves: some prepare the sulphuric acid, the nitric acid, the muriatic acid, and a few neutral salts only, in a very large way; whilst others distil oil of Turpentine, make pitch, lamp-black, &c.

The whole world is ransacked for the supply of the Chemist's elaboratory, and the Druggist's shop.

The Elaboratory is a room provided with proper conveniences for carrying on all the operations which the Chemist might choose, or have occasion for: it is generally constructed with an open chimney, in such a way, that if any unexpected explosion should take place, the ignited materials might find a ready escape. It is furnished also with suitable benches, mortars, a sand heat, a variety of glass vessels, consisting of retorts, matrasses, funnels, &c. &c. and a copper alembic, or still, for the purpose of procuring a variety of distilled waters, oils, &c. and a circular furnace for the purpose of boiling, melting, and other processes, requiring the immediate contact of fire. But, indeed, from the great variety of operations in Chemistry, we scarcely find two elaboratories alike, either in their structure, or in the different vessels which they contain. The light, however, in them all, is most desirable, when thrown down from above; and, of course, an elaboratory ought not to have any room, loft, or building over it.

The Chemist and Druggist usually makes some of his articles, even if he be only a retailer: he also sells numerous quack medicines, and frequently makes many of these when the patents have expired, or if the nostrums be known: but this is a branch of his trade by no means so reputable as could be wished, although it generally brings in a good profit, and in stamps, produces a considerable revenue to government. To sell these, an annual license must be taken out from the Stamp-Office, and a stamp of a certain value, in proportion to the value of the article sold, must be affixed to every individual phial, box, pot, or other package or inclosure.

The Chemist and Druggist generally, also, dispenses Physicians' prescriptions and by a late Act of Parliament, he is privileged so to do, without being obliged to undergo an examination at Apothecaries' Hall.

We wish that it was in our power to speak of this trade as one in which the composition of medicines was uniformly correct, and according to the directions of the *London Pharmacopaeia*; but we are sorry to say, that tales are told, which give us great reason to fear, that many unworthy persons have obtruded themselves into this respectable body; and that too much of system pervades the trade generally, for it to be quite free from the sophistication which, in medicine, is, above all things, so much to be deprecated.

Except this drawback, the preparation and sale of medicines is a very respectable line of business, and one in which, with a tolerable share of judgement, great fortunes have been made. We believe, however, that the impressions of its profitableness have directed more competitors into it, than can now find room; the profits are, in consequence, a good deal lessened, and, perhaps, its respectability impaired.

The Drug-trade, as well as the Chemist's, in the large way, is a good deal sub-divided; there are Drug merchants: those who import Drugs from abroad, and sell them to whole-sale Druggists, who sell them again to the retailer. Some of these merchants import, and sell, only particular articles.

A lad who is designed for this trade will, certainly, best succeed in it, if he is previously acquainted with the rudiments of Latin at least; and has some knowledge of Botany, and the Materia Medica. It is a trade, of all others, the most intimately connected with science. A premium of one hundred guineas is sometimes given with an apprentice. The stock in trade of a retail Chemist and Druggist, may amount to a few hundred pounds. The stock of a Chemist & Druggist, in the wholesale trade, sometimes to many thousands.

The plate represents the interior of a Chemist's elaboratory. On the left, is an alembic made of copper, with the worm tub by its side. On the right is a sand heat, with digesting bottle, retorts, receivers, &c. &c. In the middle is the furnace, where all the common operations are performed. The light is thrown from above, that being the best way in which the progress of the processes can be seen.

15

THE CONFECTIONER

A CONFECTIONER is one who makes sweetmeats, preserves of various kinds, jellies, jams, gingerbread, &c. and is generally combined with the Pastry-cook, who makes tarts, cheesecakes, pies, &c.

Confects, or confits, is a denomination given to fruits, flowers, herbs, roots, and juices, when boiled and prepared with sugar or honey to keep them, or to render them more agreeable to the taste.

The ancients only confected with honey; at present sugar is more frequently used. Confits, half sugared, are those only covered with a little sugar, to leave more of the natural taste of the fruit.

The making of gingerbread, we are told, is an art of the highest antiquity, and that its use has come to us from Asia. We read, in fact, that a bread, sweetened with honey, was made at Rhodes, of such an agreeable taste, that it could be eaten with pleasure after the most sumptuous feasts. The Greeks called this bread *melilates*: thence it came into Europe, and descending to our own times, has obtained the name of gingerbread.

Confects are reduced to eight kinds, viz. liquid confects, marmalades, jellies, pastes, dry confects, conserves, candies, and sugar-plums; sometimes called comfits.

Liquid confects are those whose fruits, either whole, in pieces, in seeds, or in clusters, are confected in a fluid, transparent syrup, which takes its colour and name from that of the fruit boiled in it. A good deal of art is necessary in preparing these well; if they be too little sugared, they will ferment and spoil, and if too much, they will candy. The most esteemed of the liquid confects, are plums, especially those called mirabels, barberries, quinces, apricots, cherries, orange-flowers, little green citrons from Madeira, green cassia from the Levant, myrobalans, ginger, cloves, &c.

Marmalades are a kind of pastes almost liquid, made of the pulp of fruits or flowers that have some consistence; such as apricots, apples, pears, plums, quinces, oranges, and ginger. Marmalade of ginger is brought from the Indies by way of Holland. It is esteemed good to revive the natural heat in aged persons.

Jellies are juices of several fruits, wherein sugar has been dissolved, and the whole, by boiling, reduced into a pretty thick consistence, so as, upon cooling, to resemble a thin transparent glue or size. Jellies are made of various kind of fruits, especially gooseberries, currants, apples, and quinces: there are other

16

jellies, made of flesh, fish, hartshorn, &c. but they are not kept long, being very subject to corrupt.

Pastes are a kind of marmalades, thickened to that degree, by a proper boiling, as to assume any form when put into little moulds, and dried in an oven. The most in use are gooseberries, quinces, apples, plums, pears, and orange-flowers; those of pistachoes are the most esteemed; those of ginger are brought from the Indies.

Dry confects are those whose fruits, after having been boiled in the syrup, are taken out again, drained, and put to dry in an oven. These are made of so many kinds of fruit, that it would be troublesome to mention them all: the most considerable are citron, lemon, and orange-peel; plums, pears, cherries, and apricots.

Conserves are a kind of dry confects, made with sugar-pastes, of flowers or fruits, &c. The most usual amongst them, are those of roses, mallows, rosemary, of hips, of orange-peel, orange-flowers, violets, jessamine, pistachoes, citrons, and sloes.

Candies are, ordinarily, entire fruits, candied over with sugar having been boiled in the syrup, which renders them like little rocks crystallized, of various figures and colours, according to the fruits enclosed in them. The best candies are brought from Italy.

Sugar-plums, or comfits, are a kind of little dry confects, made of small fruits or seeds, little pieces of bark, as cinnamon or cassia, or odoriferous and aromatic roots, &c. incrusted, and covered over with a very hard sugar ordinarily white; but sometimes of other colours. Of these there are various kinds, distinguished by various names; some are made of raspberries, others of barberries, melon seeds, pistachoes, filberts, almonds, cinnamon, cassia, orange-peel, coriander, aniseed, carraways, &c.

Ice-cream is, also, an article to be found in the Confectioner's shop; who generally lays in, during the winter, a competent supply of ice, preserved in a proper receptacle, to furnish his customers with this agreeable treat in the summer months.

The Confectioners of London are famous for the elegance and size of their Twelfth-Day cakes: for some days previously to this period, their shops are decorated with a great variety of them, made of different shapes, and with various devices upon them: some weigh many hundred pounds.

There are various forms and preparations of *gingerbread*: we shall content ourselves with giving the following recipe, which is well recommended.

Into a pound of almonds, blanched and pounded, grate a penny white loaf: sift and beat them together; to the mixture add an ounce of ginger scraped fine, and of liquorice and aniseed, in powder, of each a quarter of an ounce: pour in two or three spoonfuls of rose water, and make the whole into a paste with half a pound of sugar: mould and roll it: print it, and dry it in a stove. Some make gingerbread of treacle, citron, lemon, and orange-peel, with candied ginger, coriander, and carraway seeds, mixed up with as much flour as will make it into a paste.

The plate represents the Confectioner's shop, with jellies, sugar-plums, jams, &c.

17

THE DISTILLER

DISTILLATION is the act of dropping or falling in drops, and is more particularly applied to a process in which water, or other liquids, are placed over fire in suitable vessels, and certain parts are separated from other parts of the same liquid, by the agency of heat; it is, in every sense of the term; a chemical process.

Distillation is of considerable antiquity: of all the vessels destined to this use, the alembic is the simplest, and the most ancient. Both Dioscorides and Pliny mention the ambix, which is described by the latter of these writers: it is probably that it was, in his time, a mere plain still without any beak or gutter. The Alchemists having adopted this instrument, prefixed the Arabian article *al* to its name, and made considerable alterations in its form: the characteristic difference between an alembic and a still, seems to be in the construction of the head or capital, which, in the alembic, is contrived not merely to collect, but to condense the vapour; whereas, the corresponding part of a still, serves merely to collect the vapour which is transmitted, in an elastic state, through the beak, and condensed in the worm. Most of the French brandies, we are informed, are prepared by the alembic, properly so called, whereas all British spirits are drawn over from a still.

The English still is of a very simple construction; it is usually made of copper, and consists of a body somewhat cylindrical, and contracted at the top, called the neck, so as to admit, conveniently, the head or moveable upper part, which is contracted also, from its bellied rotundity above, into it a few inches; by which means, with proper luting, the head and body become one vessel. At the top of the head is soldered a curved tube, gradually lessening as it descends, in the shape of a swan's neck, the beak of which tube is inserted a few inches into another tube, called a *worm*, from its spiral convolutions: this juncture is, also, in distillation, closely luted. The worm is made of pewter, and is fixed in a frame in a vessel, called a worm-tub; it goes gradually descending about six times round; the upper end projecting a few inches out of the upper part of the side of the worm-tub, next the still, and the lower end projecting, also, a few inches out of the side of the lower part of the worm-tub, at a suitable distance from the still, where can be placed a proper vessel to receive the distilled product. The worm-tub is, of course, filled with water, to condense and cool the liquor as it comes over.

The still is usually, unless very small, furnished with a cock at its bottom, to draw off the remaining fluid after the distillation is effected; and is set with bricks in the same way as the common furnace for boiling liquids usually is.

We shall include Distillation and Rectification in one article, although, in this country, particularly in the metropolis and its neighbouring villages, they make two distinct trades.

The great object of the Distiller ought to be to procure a perfectly flavourless spirit, which is not an easy task. The materials for distillation, that have in this country been used in large quantities, are malt, molasses, and sugar. All these abound with an oily matter, which rising with the spirit, communicates a disagreeable flavour, from which it is with the utmost difficulty freed.

Previously to the operation of distilling, those of brewing and fermentation are necessary. Methods have been suggested, and, we believe, carried into practice, for reducing the brewing and fermentation to one operation, which are said to improve the spirit in quality, and greatly to augment its quantity. The following is the process: take ten pounds of malt, reduced to fine meal, and three pounds of common wheat-meal: add to these two gallons of water, and stir them well together; then add five gallons of water boiling-hot, and stir the whole well together. Let it stand two hours, and then stir it again; and, when grown cold, add to it two ounces of solid yeast, and set it by, loosely covered, in rather a warm place, to ferment. This is called the Dutch method of preparing what is called the wash for malt spirit. In London and its neighbourhood, the method is to draw, and mash for spirits, as is done for beer, except, that instead of boiling the wort, it is pumped into coolers, and afterwards drawn into backs to be then fermented: of course no hops are used. Thus, in the opinion of some persons, conversant with the subject, twice as much labour as is necessary is bestowed, and a large quantity of spirit is lost by leaving the gross bottoms out of the still for fear of burning.

All simple spirits may be considered in their different states of low-wines, proof-spirits, and alcohol, or rectified spirits. The first contain only one-sixth of spirit to five-sixths of water. Proof-spirits contain about one half, or rather more, of totally inflammable spirits, and alcohol, if very pure, consists wholly of spirit without any admixture or adulteration.

Malt low-wines, which is the first state after distillation from the *wash*, prepared in the usual way, are exceedingly nauseous, owing to the gross oil of the malt which abounds in it. When these are distilled gently, and by a slow-fire, into proof-spirits, they leave a considerable quantity of this foetid oil behind in the still, with the phlegm; the liquor loses its milky colour, and is clear and bright. When the proof-spirit, from malt, is distilled over again, to be brought to the state of alcohol, or rectified spirits, the utmost attention must be paid to the fire, or some of the oil will be forced over, and injure the whole process. The use of the *balneum mariae*, instead of the common still, though a much more tedious process, would effectually prevent this mischief, and give a purer spirit in one rectification, than can be procured in many, by the common methods. The *balneum mariae*, is a copper cylinder, with a bottom made to be inserted into the still, and to descend within a few inches of its bottom, so that the materials to be distilled can be placed within it, and yet have no communication with the other part of the still, which is filled two-thirds, or thereabouts, with water: the head of the still is made to fit the bath, the same as it does the still itself: by these means, a more regular and equable heat is applied to the liquor to be distilled, and which cannot be easily raised much above the boiling-point, or 212 of Fahrenheit's thermometer.

Malt spirit, and indeed spirits from other substances, must be brought into the state of alcohol, before they are adapted to internal uses; after which, they are said to be more fit for the purpose than even French brandy; but this admits of considerable doubt: French brandy containing an essential oil, or some resinous matter, which English spirits have not, that is peculiarly grateful to the stomach.

A quarter of malt will generally afford, depending upon its goodness, and the season of the year, from eight to fourteen gallons of alcohol.

The Malt Distiller always gives his spirit a single rectification, *per se* to purify it a little; in this state, though certainly not adapted to internal use, it is frequently, and at once, distilled into gin, or other ordinary compounds, for the common people; who, in this country, injure their health, and eventually destroy their constitutions by the free use of them. The Dutch never give it any further rectification than this: they distil the *wash* into low wines, and then, at once, into full-proof spirit, from which they manufacture their celebrated Holland's geneva, or gin.

The spirit loses in these processes the vinous character which it had when it came out of the hands of the Malt Distiller: the alkaline salts, used by the rectifier, uniting with the oleous and aqueous parts of the liquor, it is necessary to add an extraneous substance, to give it a flavour, and this is frequently done by sweet spirits of nitre; the common method of applying this, is by mixing it to the taste with rectified spirits. This is said to give the flavour of French brandy to our English spirits; but we think it a poor imitation, and that it is readily detected, by even indifferent judges of that liquor: other flavours are given to spirits, by putting articles into the still, so that the flavours may come over with the distilled liquor. Compound Distillers, mix with malt spirits, juniper berries, angelica root, aniseeds, turpentine, &c. and distill the whole over again, the produce of which is gin, spirit of aniseed, &c.

Rum is distilled from sugar in the West Indies; and having a great quantity of the essential oil of the sugar dissolved in it, it obtains by these means, its characteristic taste and smell. The brandy made in France, particularly in Cogniac, Bourdeaux, and Rochelle, bears the highest price: it is, in its pure state, colourless, and obtains, perhaps, its yellow tint by extracting the colouring matter from the casks in which it is kept, or more probably, it is coloured specifically by the French themselves, or by the first importers.

The Malt Distillers feed and fatten innumerable quantities of pigs upon the grains left after brewing: but the port and lard obtained from these pigs have a flabby softness about them, very different from pork fed in the usual way in the country; and, of course, do not fetch so high a price.

Spirits from sugar and molasses, are made by distilling them in water, and fermenting them in the same way as the wort from malt.

Perhaps there is no trade in the British dominions, the drug-trade excepted, which affords such facilities for fraud and adulteration; and not one in which larger fortunes have been made, we hope, to the satisfaction of the minds of those now enjoying them. A Malt Distiller requires a large capital, and much room to carry on his various operations.

Distilleries are under the close inspection and superintendence of the Board of Excise, and the proprietors of them are obliged to take out an annual license.

THE GUN MAKER

The business of the GUN-MAKER is the manufacturing of fire-arms of the smaller sorts, as muskets, fowling-pieces, pistols, &c.

The exact time when gunpowder and firearms were first employed in war by the British nation, is difficult to be discovered. If Robert Bruce may be credited, Edward the Third used cannon in his first campaign against the Scots, in 1327. The French undoubtedly used them in 1338, as well as Edward at the battle of Cressy, in 1346.

But fire-arms of a portable construction, were not, however, invented till the beginning of the sixteenth century. In 1521, the musket, mounted on a stock, was used at the siege of Parma; and, probably, was soon after adopted in England. Its form was clumsy, and its weight inconvenient; while the bow, in the hands of an English archer, retained the credit of having, within a determinate range, a steadier aim and greater execution.

The pistol had its origin from Pistoya, a town of Tuscanny, and was introduced into England, about the middle of the sixteenth century. Many of the shields, said to have been the spoils of the Armada, in 1588, have pistols in the centre, with little gratings for the aim. They were sometimes introduced at the butt-end of the pike, as well as in the time of Edward the Sixth, at the lower end of the battle-axe.

In the reign of James the First, we find muskets and calivres among the principal weapons of the infantry, as well as pistols and carabines of the cavalry. The great alteration when matchlocks were no longer used, took place about the third or fourth year of William the Third.

The progress of fire-arms in France, was not dissimilar to that of England. It was not till after the accession of Francis the First, in 1515, that any considerable change was effected. Between that time and the death of Henry the Third, in 1589, pikes, the ancient weapon of the French infantry, gave place to the arquebuss; while in the cavalry, lances were gradually and reluctantly exchanged for the pistol. At that period, the Spaniards were far superior to the French in the art of war. The infantry of Philip the Second, by whom the use of fire-arms was very early adopted, spread terror over Europe.

The principal part of the muskets, fowling-pieces, pistols, &c. is the barrel, which, however, is not made by those who call themselves Gun-Smiths, but by persons who forge them in a large way, and who have forges and premises adapted to the business; the forges used by Gun-Smiths being on a much smaller scale than those required for the manufacture of the barrels.

Amongst Gun-Smiths, great attention is paid to the division of labour: one man or set of men, is employed in what is termed the boring, though, in truth, the barrels are formed at first with a bore throughout, but not with that accuracy which is required for these kind of instruments; other persons are employed to file and polish the outside of the barrel; to some is allotted the business of making and fixing the breech, the touch-hole, &c. others, forge the locks in a rough way, and others are employed to file, polish, and put together the several parts of which the locks are composed.

The barrel ought to possess the following properties: *lightness*, that it may be as portable as possible, and *strength*, to bear the effect of a full charge without bursting; it ought to be constructed, so as not to recoil with violence, and it ought to be of sufficient length, to carry the bullet to as great a distance as the force of the powder employed is capable of doing.

To form a gun-barrel in the manner generally practised for those denominated common, the workmen begin by heating and hammering out a bar of iron into the form of a flat ruler, thinner at the end intended for the muzzle, and thicker at that for the breech: the length, breadth, and thickness of the whole plate being, of course, regulated by the intended length, diameter, and weight of the barrel. This oblong plate of metal, is then by repeated beating and hammering, turned round a cylindrical rod of tempered iron, called a mandril, whose diameter is considerably less than the intended bore of the barrel. The edges of the plate are made to overlap each other about half an inch, and are welded together by heating the tube in lengths of two or three inches at a time, and hammering it with very brisk but moderate strokes upon an anvil which has a number of semicircular furrows upon it, adapted to the various sizes of barrels. The heat required for welding, is the bright white heat which precedes fusion, and at which the particles of the iron unite so intimately with one another, than when properly managed no trace is left of their former separation. These heatings and hammerings are repeated until the whole barrel has undergone the same operation, and all its parts are rendered as perfectly continuous as if it had been bored out of a solid piece. For better work, the barrel is forged in separate pieces, of eight or nine inches in length, and then welded together, lengthways, as well as in the lapping over. The other mode being the easiest and quickest done, is the most usual.

The barrel is now either finished in the common manner, or made to undergo the operation of twisting, which is a process commonly employed on those barrels which are intended to be of a superior quality and price. This operation consists in heating the barrel in portions of a few inches at a time to a high degree of red heat; when one end of it is screwed into a vice, and into the other is introduced a square piece of iron with a handle like an auger, and by means of these the fibres of the heated portion are twisted in a spiral direction, which is thought to resist the efforts of the powder much better than a longitudinal one.

Pistol-barrels, which are to go in pairs, are forged in one piece, and are cut asunder at the muzzles after they have been bored; by which, there is not only a saving of iron and labour, but a certainty of the calibre being the same in both.

The next operation consists in boring; this is done in the following manner: two beams of strong wood, as oak, each of about six inches in diameter, and six or seven feet long, are placed horizontally and parallel to each other, having their extremities mortised upon a strong upright piece about three feet high, and firmly fixed. A space of from two to four inches is left between the horizontal pieces, in which a piece of wood is made to slide, by having at each end a tenon let into a groove, which runs on the inside of each beam throughout its whole length. Through this sliding piece, a pin, or bolt of iron, is driven or screwed in a perpendicular direction, having at its upper end, a round hole large enough to admit the breech of the barrel, which is secured on it by means of a piece of iron, that serves as a wedge, and a vertical screw passing through the upper part of the hole. A chain is fastened to a staple on one side of the sliding piece, which runs between the two horizontal beams, and passing over a pulley at one end of the machine, has a weight hooked to it. An upright piece of timber is fixed above this pulley, between the end of the beams, having its upper end perforated by the axis of an iron crank, furnished with a square socket; the other axis being supported by the wall on a strong post, and loaded with a heavy wheel of cast iron, to give it force. The axes of the crank are in a line with the hole in the bolt already described. The borer being then fixed into the socket of the crank, has its other end previously well oiled, introduced into the barrel whose breech part is made fast in the hole of the bolt; the chain is then carried over the pulley and the weight hooked on; the crank being then turned with the hand, the barrel advances as the borer cuts its way, till it has passed through the whole length.

The *boring bit* is a rod of iron somewhat longer than the barrel, one end being made to fit the socket of the crank, and the other being furnished with a cylindrical plug of tempered steel about an inch and a half in length, and having its surface cut in the manner of a perpetual screw. A number of bits, each a little larger than the preceding one, are afterwards passed successively through the barrel in the same way, until it has acquired the intended calibre.

The last operation is that of colouring the barrel, previously to which it is polished with fine emery and oil, until it presents to the eye, throughout its whole length, a perfectly smooth and even surface. The practice of blueing, is now discontinued, and browning is adopted in its stead. To do this, the barrel is rubbed over with nitric, or sulphuric acid, diluted with water, and laid by until a coat of rust is formed upon it, more or less according to the colour wanted; a little oil is then applied, and the surface being rubbed dry, it is polished by means of a hard-brush and bees-wax.

The proving of barrels differs in different countries. The English Tower proof, and that of the Whitechapel company, incorporated by charter for proving arms, are made with a ball of the proper calibre, and a charge of powder equal in weight to this ball: the proof is the same for every size and species of barrel, and not repeated.

Rifling consists in forming upon the inside of barrels a number of furrows, either in a straight or spiral direction; into these, the ball is moulded, and any rolling motion along the sides of the barrel in its passage out is thereby prevented. This process is supposed to direct the ball more effectually to the object against which it is intended to operate. Barrels of this construction have been long in use upon the Continent, but were little known, and still less employed in England, till within these fifty years.

On the upper surface of the barrel, at right angles with its axis, is fixed a piece of flat, thin iron, about six inches from the breech, and on the centre of its top, a small square notch is filed; this is called the back-sight. The front-sight is nothing more than the small iron knot which is fixed on all fowling-pieces about half an inch from the muzzle. When the aim is taken, the eye is raised over the back-sight till the front-sight appears through the notch, which is then brought upon the object.

Great care is taken in the manufacture and finishing of the gun-lock: it consists of divers parts, such as the cock which holds the flint, the priming-pan to hold a small quantity of powder, which is connected by the touch-hole with that in the barrel; the hammer, which covers the priming, and against the upper part of which the flint strikes; the trigger, used to bring the flint and hammer in contact; and certain springs, as the main-spring, the rear-spring, &c. which are concealed in the stock, and which are adapted either to hold the cock on the half-cock, whole-cock, or to extricate it at the moment of firing the piece.

Improvements upon gun-locks to prevent their going off accidentally, have latterly been made; and Mr. Manton, of Dorset Street, has obtained a patent for one upon improved principles: but we doubt whether any effectual improvement could be adopted, consistent with the simplicity required in this destructive weapon.

The lock is let into the gun-stock, which is uniformly manufactured from the wood of the walnut-tree, of which the Gun-Smith always keeps a large stock, and well seasoned. The gun-stocks are usually made by workmen at their own homes, because one man will fashion gun-stocks sufficient for the wants of several Gun-Smiths.

Before any of the pieces described are appropriated for service, it is necessary, as we have already observed, that each barrel should undergo a particular trial of its soundness, to be made by or before a persons authorized for the purpose, called the Proof-master.

Gun-flints are made in large quantities, both in France and England, from the nodules of flint found in various places, particularly in chalk districts. The whole operation of making a gun-flint is performed in less than one minute. A good workman is able to manufacture a thousand good chips, or scales, in a day, if the flint nodules be of a good quality: and in the same manner he can fashion five hundred gun-flints in a day; so that in the space of three days, he is able to clean and finish a thousand gun-flints without farther assistance. The gun-flints are sorted out according to their perfection. They are classed into extra and common flints; flints for pistols, muskets, and fowling pieces.

The
Hat Maker
from
Volume I

The
Apothecary
from
Volume I

The Straw Hat
Maker
from
Volume I

The
Tallow Chandler
from
Volume I

The
Cutler
from
Volume II

The
Cork Cutter
from
Volume II

The
Ladies'
Dress-maker
from
Volume II

The
Tin-plate
Worker
from Volume II

THE LINEN DRAPER

THE LINEN-DRAPER sells cloths which are made of flax and hemp; as Irish linens, Russia towelling, Cambrics, &c. and, also, shawls, printed calicoes, muslin, &c. &c.

This business must have been in a great degree coeval with the subdivision of labour, arising from civilization, modified, of course, by a variety of circumstances. In London, it is, in the number of its articles, much more circumscribed than it is in the country. Linen-Drapers frequently, in the country, combining with their trade that of a Silk-Mercer, whereas, in London, these two trades are wholly distinct.

The Linen-Draper is now comprehended under two, or at most, three distinct branches. We have the *Linen-merchant*, a person whose more immediate province it is to import articles of linen manufacture from foreign countries, such as Irish cloths from Ireland, a variety of cloths made of hemp and flax, from Russia, Ticklenburghs, &c. from Germany, and nankins, calicoes, muslins, &c. from the East Indies.

We have, also, the *wholesale Linen-Draper*; a person whose business is to purchase linens from the merchant, and muslins, calicoes, printed-cottons, &c. from the different manufacturers in Manchester, Blackburn, Paisley, &c. and to sell them to the retail Linen-Drapers throughout the kingdom, as well as frequently for exportation. For this purpose, the *wholesale* Linen-Draper generally keeps one or two, or more persons, constantly travelling throughout the country with patterns of his various articles, by which means, the retail dealer has an opportunity of choosing his goods without the expensive and troublesome process of a journey to London, or some other great market for that purpose. The business now done, or rather which lately was done in this way, is beyond all precedent or calculation.

The most striking part, however, is the *retail* Linen-Draper. We believe there is no trade in England, in which more efforts are made to captivate the public, and more especially the ladies, by a display of goods; and in London, this display is carried to a most costly and sumptuous extent. In most of the principal streets of the metropolis, shawls, muslins, pieces for ladies' dresses, and a variety of other goods, are shown with the assistance of mirrors, and at night by chandeliers, aided by the brilliancy which the gas-lights afford, in a way almost as dazzling to a stranger, as many of those poetical fictions of which we read in the Arabian nights' entertainment.

If, some years ago, our neighbours in sneer, called us a nation of shopkeepers, we think that they must now give us the credit of being shopkeepers of taste; we apprehend, no place in the world affords so great a variety of elegant amusement to the eye, as London in its various shops, and amongst these, those of the Linen-Draper are at all times conspicuous.

One of the principal things in this trade, in order to be able to carry it on with success, is a knowledge of the best markets for purchasing the different articles of which a Linen-Draper's shop is made up: it may seem that immediate application to the fountain head, the manufacturers in various parts of the country, would be the best, but experience has frequently decided otherwise; and it is now well known, that from a variety of circumstances, linen and cotton goods can be often purchased in London, cheaper than of the manufacturers themselves. The truth, perhaps, is, that the greatest quantity of floating capital is always to be found in the metropolis, and, therefore, the manufacturer will send his goods to that market, where they will be sure to obtain a ready sale, and that too, generally, for prompt payment, or for bills at a short date. Large sales, therefore, of muslin, calicoes, &c. are, in London, numerous, and the capitalist is generally sure of purchasing well. Hence it in general happens, that no wholesale Linen-Draper, residing in any other part of the empire, can effectually compete with the London houses: and this has been particularly the case for some years past, owing to the peculiarly depressed state of trade.

At *Manchester*, are manufactured printed calicoes, checks, muslins, nankins, jeans, &c.

At *Blackburn*, white calicoes are the staple commodity. At *Wigan*, is manufactured a particular kind of check, known by its name, *wigan*, of strong and durable quality.

At Bristol, Birmingham, and various other places, white calicoes are also manufactured.

In Somersetshire, *bed-tick* of fine quality, and *dowlas*, are manufactured of a superior strength to most; *Yeovil, Langport*, and their neighbourhoods, are the chief seats of these manufactures: fairs in some of the towns of the county, are held for the sale of these articles annually, and, indeed, oftener.

Paisley, in Scotland, has latterly become eminent as a mart for printed cottons, calico, check, muslin, cambric, &c. &c.

Yorkshire has, also, its linen manufacture, and in the articles called huckaback and sheeting, it is well known.

London is, principally, in this trade, noted for getting up the most elegant articles in the printed calico and muslin departments; distinguished in the trade by the name of *London prints*.

Some of the retail Linen-Drapers in the metropolis, transact daily, so much business, as almost to exceed belief: there seems a disposition in the public to go to what are termed cheap shops, many of which have a name for doing business well, which, if conducted with any degree of prudence, soon insure a fortune. We have known persons in this line, whose receipts have averaged five hundred pounds per day, for a long period. In such a shop, twenty or thirty persons, or more, are constantly employed, the average of whose salaries do not amount to forty pounds a year, exclusive of their board: of course, a small per centage on three thousands pounds a week, will cover those expenses, and afford a good profit also. We cannot, however, avoid considering these overgrown and engrossing houses as a very great evil; but we suppose that, as long as the British public are actuated by real or pretended cheapness, these houses must continue to monopolize the profits which would be more advantageous to the community, if considerably subdivided.

This is a business in which, we believe, more persons have failed than in any other in the united kingdom, owing to its being liable to partake of the fluctuations, unfortunately almost inherent in the manufacturing system, and to the great versatility in fashion and dress. It is a trade too in which, we are sorry to say, there is a trick at which the cheek of honesty cannot fail to redden, but which is become so common, as almost to be identified with the trade itself: we mean the bad practice of asking various prices for the same article, the same quantity of it, and on the same day, depending, in a great measure, upon the opinion which the shopman happens to conceive of the sagacity of his customer.

In this trade, in every branch, a considerable capital is generally required. Apprentice fees vary exceedingly: they are sometimes one hundred guineas; but more commonly, young men make their way in this business without any fee at all. Experienced shopmen get, sometimes, fifty or sixty pounds a year, and their board. We have known wholesale travellers, who were clever men and had good connexions, receive two hundred pounds a year as a salary.

The plate represents the interior of a retail Linen-Draper's shop in one of the most frequented streets of the metropolis.

THE LOOKING-GLASS MAKER

THE LOOKING-GLASS MAKER is a person who lays tin foil on polished pieces of glass, by the assistance of quicksilver, so as to produce reflection by effectually obstructing the rays of light, and, afterwards, fits the glass to frames of various sizes, either for the use of chambers and dressing-rooms, or for the purpose of decoration in the houses and mansions of the opulent.

Nature offered to mankind the first mirrors, in representing objects upon the surface of water when it was still. Human industry and ingenuity has, from time to time, improved upon such suggestions, and has not only equalled, but very far exceeded the original model. The discovery of metals considerably assisted man in the progress of this art. Mirrors were at first made of polished brass, of tin, or of burnished iron, and, also, of a mixture of tin and brass. A person named Praxiteles, not the sculptor of that name, who was contemporary with Pompey the Great, made mirrors of silver. These last were preferred to all the other kinds, and the use of them was only abandoned, when glass coated with tin, as we now have it, was introduced.

The precise time in which the ancients began to use glass for mirrors is not known: the first, we think, was furnished from the glass-houses of Sidon, where glass was worked in a variety of ways, both for use and ornament. As to the stone which the Romans adapted to their windows, in order to keep out the rain and weather, it does not appear that they ever employed it as mirrors.

In the thirteenth century, the Venetians were the only people who had the art of making looking-glasses of crystal. The great glass works at Murano, in the neighbourhood of Venice, furnished all Europe for centuries, with the finest glasses that were made. The first plates for looking-glasses were made in England, at Lambeth, in 1673, by the encouragement of the Duke of Buckingham, who in 1670 introduced a few Venetian artists.

The polishing of the plates for this business is usually effected by other hands, before they come to the Looking-Glass Maker, but we can just mention, that the usual mode of making glass smooth, and in every respect proper to receive the tin foil and quicksilver, is to use first of all, fine sand and water, then emery of different degrees of fineness; and, lastly, colcothar of vitriol or as it is more commonly called, crocus martis, or purple brown. The polishing instrument is a block of wood, covered with several folds of cloth and carded wool, so as to make a fine elastic cushion. This block is worked by the hand; but, to increase the pressure of the polisher, the handle is lengthened by a wooden spring, bent to a bow three or four feet long, which, at the other extremity, rests against a fixed point to a beam placed above. The plate is now fastened to a table with plaister, covered with colcothar, and the polisher begins his operation by working it backwards and forwards over the surface of the plate till one side is done; then the other is to be polished in the same manner.

It is well known, that glass when smoothed and polished, does not acquire the property of reflecting objects till it has been silvered, as it is called, an operation effected by means of an amalgam of tin and quicksilver. The tin-leaf, or as it is more commonly called, tin-foil, which is employed for the purpose, must be of the same size as the glass, because when pieces of that metal are united by means of mercury, they exhibit the appearance of lines. Tin is one of those metallic substances which become soonest oxydated by admixture with mercury. If there remain a portion of the oxyde of a blackish grey colour on the leaf of tin, it produces a spot, or stain in the mirror, and that part cannot reflect objects presented to it: great care, therefore, must be taken in silvering glass, to remove whatever portion of oxyde there might be from the surface of the amalgam.

The process is as follows: the tin-foil is laid on a very smooth stone table, usually prepared for the purpose, with grooves on its edges, or with ledges to preserve the waste quicksilver, and mercury being poured over the metal, it is extended over the surface of it, by means of a rubber made of bits of cloth. At the same moment, the surface of the tin foil becomes covered with blackish oxyde, which must be removed with the rubber. More mercury is then to be poured over the tin, where it remains at a level to the thickness of more than a line, without running off. The glass must be applied in a horizontal direction to the table at one of its extremities, and being pushed forwards, it drives before it the oxide of tin, which is at the surface of the amalgam. A number of leaden weights covered with cloth, are then placed on the glass, which floats on the amalgam, in order to press it down. Without this precaution, the glass would exhibit the interstices of the crystals resulting from the amalgam: in this state, it is generally suffered to remain several days, till the mixture adheres firmly to the glass.

To obtain leaves of tin, which are, sometimes, six or seven feet in length, with a proportionate breadth, they are not rolled, but hammered after the manner of gold-beaters. The prepared tin is first cast between two plates of polished iron, or between two smooth stones, not of a porous nature. Twelve of these plates are placed over each other; and they are then beaten on a stone with heavy hammers, one side of which is plain, the other rounded. The plates joined together, are first beaten with the latter: when they become extended, the number of plates is doubled, so that they amount, sometimes, to eighty or more. They are then smoothed with the flat side of the hammer, and are beaten till they acquire the length of six or seven feet, and the breath of four or five. The small block of tin from which they are formed, is at first ten inches long, six in breadth, and a line and a quarter in thickness. When the leaves are of a less extent and thin, from eighty to a hundred of them are smoothed together.

This is a trade which is, comparatively, in very few hands, and is, in consequence, one of considerable profit: it is, however, not always carried on alone, but is often combined with that of a carver and gilder; some cabinet-makers also undertake it.

THE MACHINIST

If any thing is capable of persuading man that he is of a superior order of being to that of the animals which surround him, it is above all the beauty of his inventions and the inexhaustible resources which he find in his industry. He is born weak and absolutely naked. His weakness renders him even active and industrious. Upon a contemplation of his own poverty, he calls into activity all his senses. He applies force to force, opposition to resistance - velocity to weight - and weight to velocity. By the assistance of Mechanics this little being of five or six feet in height, with two arms, can expedite as much work as a giant whom we might imagine having a thousand. Take Mechanics from man, and you reduce him to barren thought. Mechanics have done what there is of most beautiful upon the earth.

The Machinist who embodies in his profession the chief principles of Mechanics, and brings them into active use, is the follower of an occupation of very recent introduction amongst the social and useful arts. It is true, we had to a remote period the common smith, the founder, and the carpenter; and the optician has also been for some time known; but such has been the rapid improvement in mechanical machinery during the last fifty years, that the Machinist was wanting to unite the correct precision of the finer branches of Mechanics to the practical utilities of the common smith, the carpenter, &c.

As the *steam engine* occupies so conspicuous a portion in this trade, indeed, is the chief moving power in it, we deem it necessary to say, that it is, unquestionably, one of the noblest monuments of human ingenuity. It was originally invented by the Marquis of Worcester, in the reign of Charles the Second. This nobleman published in 1663, a small book called "A Century of Inventions", giving an account of a hundred different discoveries or contrivances of his own, amongst these, is an account of raising water by the force of steam, which, now that we are possessed of the engine, appears to agree very well with its construction. But as there was no plate accompanying his description, we are entirely unacquainted with the particular mode in which he applied the power of steam. It does not appear, however, that he met with sufficient encouragement, and this useful discovery was long neglected.

Towards the end of the seventeenth century, Captain Savary succeeded in constructing a machine of this kind, having, probably, seen the Marquis of Worcester's account; obtained a patent for the invention, and erected several steam engines which he described in a book entitled the "Miner's Friend," published in 1696.

In the beginning of the eighteenth century, Newcomen and Crauly first conceived the project of applying a piston with a lever and other machinery. They were contented to share the profits of the invention with Savary, who procured a patent for it in 1705, in which they all three joined. But it was not till 1712, that the difficulties in working it were removed.

About 1762, Mr. Watt began to turn his attention to this machine, which he has since brought to so great a degree of perfection.

Perhaps we cannot better describe the trade of a Machinist than in enumerating some of the most important articles which he manufactures, which are, machinery constructed and manufactured for experimental and scientific elucidation, steam engines, both of condensing and high pressure to any required power. Digesters, chemical apparatus, philosophical and gas-light machines; conductors for protecting buildings and shipping from lightning. Pumps both atmospheric and forcing, machines for soda and artificial water; syphons, air and fluid cocks; exhausting and condensing syringes; garden engines, fountains, hydrostatic engines, and hydro-mechanical presses, cutting engines for screws; wheels, cylinders, and boring bars, stamping and cutting presses with dies and punches. Saw-mills, portable iron forges, mill work, and large framing in wood and iron. Mechanical modelling and experimental machinery. Turning lathes, lead and pewter pipe moulds, all sorts of turning in iron, steel, and brass, with screw cutting, and a great variety of other articles for mechanical movements, which it would not be easy to enumerate.

It is obvious, that the person who carries on this business must be possessed of considerable ingenuity and great mechanical knowledge: his employment being of a very complicated kind. He requires the talents and experience of the joiner, the brass and iron founder, the smith and the turner, in their most extended variety. It is by uniting the power of these several occupations into one, together with the great assortment of excellent tools which he unavoidably requires, that the Machinist is furnished with those facilities of manufacture which peculiarly belong to his employment. The saw, the plane, the chisel and the hammer; the furnace, and all the implements for casting; the forge, the anvil, the vice; and the products of these tools are, at last, submitted to the *turning lathe*. This machine, and its apparatus, as they are now found in the Machinist's manufactory, form the grand and rapid instrument that, by the assistance of the steam engine to give it motion, produces the accuracy which we find in all the different machinery and instruments that the Machinist prepares.

The *turning lathe*, and its various applications, would occupy much more space than we can spare to describe: we can only hint at them. Cylinders, both interior and exterior, are turned and bored; plain surfaces of any form, are smoothed; cones, globes, and every other figure that the skill of the workman or the ingenuity of the apparatus can effect, are brought to their exact shape and polish by this machine, which ranks above all others in usefulness, as well as in the endless variety of its powers.

The plate represents the Machinist's workshop; with the five mechanical powers, viz. the screw, the pulley, the wheel, the wedge, and the lever. There is, also, the turning lathe, the steam engine, and the saw mill.

Able journeymen at this business, will get from thirty to fifty shillings per week.

We have obtained the principal part of this description from an inspection of the workshop of Mr. Alexander Galloway, the Machinist, No. 69, High Holborn, who, we understand, was the first person who established himself under this designation, and who is a proof, in his own person, of the great power, activity, and ingenuity of man.

THE MUSICAL INSTRUMENT MAKER

THE MUSICAL INSTRUMENT-MAKER requires no further definition than that which the name itself imports.

Music, as well as painting, can be traced to the most remote antiquity. The most savage nations are not strangers to the pleasure which it affords. We find in every country, the art more or less perfect, the instruments more or less rude, in proportion to the degree of civilization to which the people have arrived.

After the ordinary exercise of speech, to express our wants, and our intentions, it is a great pleasure to hear from the same voice, a melodious song, and this melody is frequently such, that the most perfect instruments are still, in expression, far below it.

However, the art and ingenuity of man have now brought musical instruments to a surprising degree of perfection, and considerably added to the elegant luxuries and refinements of the age.

It will be impossible for us to mention all the instruments which are made, either of the wind or stringed kind, but we shall describe some of the principal ones, in order to give some idea of the whole, and of the trade of which we now treat.

The *organ* is an instrument of the highest antiquity, in the structure of which the greatest ingenuity has been displayed. The most difficult part of this instrument in its manufacture, is the wind chest, which is a large horizontal box, so closely fitted and prepared as to retain the wind forced into it, by various large bellows, which must be numerous, and capacious in proportion to the size of the wind chest. The quantity of wind in it is always known to the organist, by means of a tell-tale or index attached to the bellows, which rises and falls in proportion to the quantity of air, and apprizes the performer in what degree the wind is exhausted. The top of the wind chest is bored with several lines of apertures, proportioned to the sizes of the pipes which they are to receive, those of the bass notes being of course the largest; but all the pipes in each row being different as to their interior construction, and consequently producing very different sounds, each row is called a *stop*, and has a plug appropriate to it, acting upon a slide, which shuts or opens the whole of that row at pleasure; this is called a register. There are as many of such rows of apertures, or registers, as there are kinds of tones, or stops on the organ: some having few, others having numerous stops. The wind is prevented from escaping from the wind chest, into the pipes by valves, which are opened only when the performer presses the keys respectively: when, by means, of communicating wires, the valves are pressed down, and the wind passes into the pipes. When the key is quitted, the pressure of the wind, aided by a spiral wire-spring, shuts the valve, and the sound of that pipe instantly ceases. In order to regulate the force of the sound, most church-organs have either two or three rows of keys whereby a greater or less number of pipes may be filled, and the powers of the instrument be controlled into what is called the small organ or be let loose, so as to become the full organ. The pipes suited to the higher notes, are made of mixed metals, chiefly tin and lead; they increase in length and diameter, in proportion to the note; until metal pipes being no farther applicable, square ones of wood are substituted in their stead, for all the lower notes. The dimensions of all the pipes of an organ, are regulated by a scale or diapason, formed for the use of the manufacturers in this line and apportioned to every size of the instrument usually made.

The *stops* usually made in a great organ, are the *open diapason*, in which all the pipes are open at the top; this is a metallic stop: - the *stopped diapason*, the bass-notes of which, up to the tenor C, are always made of wood, and are stopped at their summits, with wooden plugs, by which the tone is very much softened: - the *principal* is the middle stop, which serves, when tuned, as the basis for tuning all the other parts, above and below; it is metallic: - the *twelfth*, which is metallic also, derives its name from being a twelfth, or an octave and a half above the diapason; the *fifteenth*, so called because it is two octaves above the diapason; the *sesquialtera* is composed of various pipes, turned in the parts of the common chord; the upper part is often called the cornet; - the furniture stop is very shrill, and in some passages has a peculiarly fine effect; the *trumpet* is a metallic stop, and derives its name from the instrument which it so admirably imitates; this peculiar tone is produced by what is called a reed, but in reality a piece of brass, on which the wind acts forcibly, giving a roughness of sound, which is further changed by all the pipes of this stop having bell mouths like trumpets; the *clarion* is a reed-stop also, but an octave higher than the trumpet: the *tierce* is a third above the fifteenth. The octave above the twelfth is too shrill to be used, but in the full organ; the *cornet* is a treble stop: the *dulcimer* takes its name from the sweetness of its sound; there are also the *flute*, the *bassoon, vox-humana, haut-boy,* and *cremona* stops.

The fingering of an organ is precisely the same as that of the piano-forte, so far as relates to the situation of the keys, &c.: but on account of the great number of holding notes in organ music, the fingers are never kept down, whence it is considered highly injudicious to piano-forte performers to practice the organ, they being subject to lose that lightness, and that delicacy of touch required for the former instrument.

Organs are also made with barrels, on which are a great number of pins, and staples, of flat brass wire, and of different lengths. The barrel being turned by means of a cranker winch, the wires that communicate with the valves in the wind-chest, are acted upon by the pins and staples, which hold down the valves for a longer or shorter time, according to the duration of the notes, which they are designed to give. On these barrels, which are made to shift at pleasure, from ten to fifteen tunes are usually made. The winch not only turns the barrel, but also works a pair of bellows, by which the wind chest is supplied. This instrument is called the hand, or barrel organ, and is very common in the streets of London.

Before we quit the organ, we may just observe, and the observation will be equally applicable to the manufacturers of other musical instruments, that the organ-builder should possess a nice, accurate, and highly cultivated ear, and a sound judgement, in the vibratory qualities of wood and metal. He should also be acquainted with the science of pneumatics, and practical mechanics; and he should be so far informed in the simple elements of musical composition, as to be capable of trying the different stops and combinations of his own instruments, and of deciding for himself, on the effects in performance.

Having been so diffuse in the account of the organ, our notice of the other instruments must be somewhat circumscribed. But we may remark generally, that in the structure of all kinds of musical instruments, both wind and stringed, the use of well seasoned wood is of the utmost importance, and that to the preparing and seasoning it, the attention of the musical instrument manufacturer must be particularly directed: for with every precaution in this particular, from the alterations of the atmosphere, the best instruments will sometimes get out of tune; and, with neglect, the artist's labour will often be in vain.

The other principal wind Instruments, now in use are, the mouth-organ, or *Pandean-pipes*, frequently played as an accompaniment to other music in the streets; they consist of a range of pipes, bound together, side by side, gradually lessening with respect to each other in diameter, and shortening in length. The longest is about six inches, and the shortest about two inches in length.

The *Eolian harp* consists of a long box, in which four or more strings are stretched its whole length, and tuned to the component parts of any common chord, such as, C.E.G. C.E.G. &c. opposite the line of strings, which are placed over a slanting sounding board, and two slits, one on each side, running parallel with the entire strings, or a circular hole with ornamental openings, is made in the centre of the box, under the strings; when this instrument is placed in a confined passage, a window for example, the air rushing between the strings, and through the apertures in the box, produces a variety of harmonious and beautiful sounds.

The *Trumpet* may be next mentioned. It is made of metal: those of silver are by far the softest in tone, but brass is in general use. It has a mouth-piece, about an inch in diameter, concave for the lips to act within, and closing to a very narrow tube. Trumpets with slides to lower or raise the pitch one or two notes, are the best and most useful instrument of this class.

The *French Horn* consists of a long tube twisted into several circular folds, gradually increasing in diameter, from the end at which it is blown, to that at which the wind issues. Those intended for concerts, have like the trumpets, various crooks, and a slide, whereby they may be brought to accord with the most scrupulous exactness.

The *Serpent* is so called from its form: its mouth-piece is very similar to that of the trumpet, but it is made of ivory. This is the deepest bass instrument of all that have five finger holes. It is made of very thin wood, covered with buckram and leather, so as to become very firm.

In the *common flute* there are seven fingers above, and one for each thumb below; some have only one thumb hole, other two small ones: the sound is generated by blowing through a slit into the bore, the superfluous wind passing out at a vent made on the top close to the upper end. All the flageolet tribe, which are of various sorts and sizes, belong to this species; one lately introduced, called the double flageolet, is a very pleasing instrument.

The *German-flute* is also a very agreeable instrument, it is usually made of box, or some very hard and seasoned wood.

The *Bassoon* is not, we believe, so much in use as it formerly was. It has two bodies and a swan neck brass tube, with a reed attached to it, through which the sound is generated.

The *Hautboy* and *Clarionet* have mouth pieces of different forms, made of reeds, or canes.

The principal varieties of stringed instruments are found in the harp, the piano-forte, the guitar, the violin, and the Eolian harp, before mentioned, &c.

In the *Harp*, each note has a separate string; in the Welsh harp, there are two strings to each note of the principal scale, with an intermediate row for the semitones. In the pedal harp, the half notes are formed, by pressing pins against the strings, so as to shorten their effective length.

In the *Harpsichord* and *Spinnet*, instruments gone very much out of fashion, the quill acts like the finger in the harp, or the plectrum in the lyre.

In the *Piano-forte* the sound is produced by a blow of a hammer, raised by a lever, which is as much detached from it as possible. The *Grand Piano* resembles the harpsichord in form, but its action and tone, are much superior. Its wires run longitudinally along the belly, or sounding board, supported at about two-thirds of an inch distance by small, low, carved battens of beech, or other wood, into which pins are firmly driven, for the purpose of keeping the wires perfectly parallel. These battens, called bridges, determine the lengths of the several wires; though the latter pass beyond them for some distance, being hooked on at their farther ends, to stout pins driven into a solid part of the frame-work, and coming over the bridge, which is next to the keys, with which it is parallel, and winding on a set of iron pegs, which, being driven into a solid block of hard wood, are turned either right or left, by means of a small instrument, called a *tuning hammer*, and are thus tightened or relaxed at pleasure. The shortest wires are the thinnest, which lie to the right, and give the upper notes: the longest are to the left, and give the lowest notes; those between them are longer or shorter according to their vibration, their several lengths increasing as they approach towards the left side of the instrument, forming, by means of the bridges, which lie obliquely, a triangular figure. Each note has three wires lying within, somewhat less than half an inch in breadth: these are equidistant, and proceed to three rows of tuning-pins, so that the tuner cannot mistake as to which of the three wires he acts upon. The wires are imported from Germany, our artisans not having acquired the mode of giving them a due degree of temper. Those of the higher notes are of brass, and commonly begin with no. 8, 9, or 10, gradually increasing in thickness, until they reach the extent of about four octaves, when they give place to copper wires, which produce a deeper sound.

Most grand piano-fortes have two pedals, one for each foot, communicating with the interior; one is designed to raise all the dampers completely, the other to throw the whole of the key-frame to the right, more or less; by which means the hammers are slid at the same moment in a body, about a quarter of an inch to the right, also so as to quit either one or two, at pleasure, of the left hand wires of each note, and to strike upon only one or two, as is judged proper for the greater or less diminution of sound. The sounding board, or belly, is made of very fine narrow deals, chiefly imported from the continent, and so closely joined, that in many, no line or indication of junction, can be distinguished.

The square piano-forte is very different in form from the grand. It however, has an action and movements nearly similar.

The *Piano-forte* is of German origin, and derives its name from its equal command, both of softness and strength of tone.

The *Guitar* is played with the fingers like the Harp. It has a broad neck, on which are various frets, made of wires, fixed into the finger board, at right angles with the wires; these being the guides for the fingers to make the several notes by passing between the frets. The bridge is very low, and stands behind a circular sound-hole, covered with an ornamental and perforated plate; the body of the guitar is of an oval form, the sides perpendicular to the belly and back.

The *Violin* is an instrument universally known. All the violin class have four strings fastened at one end to a small piece of ebony, called the tail-piece, and after passing over a raised bridge, made of seasoned wood, and over a little ridge, called the nut, are fastened respectively to four pegs, made of very hard tough wood, by the turning of which the strings are put in tune. All the strings give fifths to their neighbours throughout; thus the first string is E; the second A, the third D; and the fourth, which is a covered one, is G; the tenors and basses have no E string, but a C one added below the G. The notes are made by compressing the strings on a rounded slip of ebony, called a finger board, which proceeds from the nut, full four-fifths of the distance between that and the bridge, the latter being always placed on the belly or sounding board, exactly between the centres of the two sound holes, which are in the form of an S; the belly is supported by a small piece of rounded deal, called the sounding post, without which the tones would be imperfect and harsh.

Violin strings were formerly obtained from Rome, Naples, and some parts of Germany; but latterly they have been manufactured in England, of equal quality with those procured from abroad.

Of *Drums* we have an abundant variety. The side or military drum, is well known. The *Kettle* drum derives its name from its form, the bottom being made of copper, and the head being vellum, or goat's skin.

The *Tabor* is a small drum, so flat, that the two heads are not more than three inches asunder.

The *Tambourine* is a kind of drum, with only one head, the other end of the hoop, which is not more than four inches in breadth, being open.

The *Triangle* is known from its name; but we must not swell our article with any further notice.

The business of a Musical Instrument Maker is a very lucrative one. The trade in Piano-fortes alone is one of considerable magnitude, seventy guineas being frequently paid for a good article of this kind. The price of an organ frequently amounts to many hundred pounds. Of course considerable capital is necessary in this trade, and the wages of journeymen are good.

The Plate represents the musical instrument-maker's shop.

THE OPTICIAN

The Optician makes telescopes, microscopes, spectacles, opera-glasses, reading glasses, &c. &c.

The history of this important art will, in effect, be an account of the art itself, which we shall endeavour to give in as concise and perspicuous a manner as we can, consistent with the design of this work.

Although the ancients made few optical experiments, they nevertheless knew that when light passed through media of different densities, it did not move in a straight line, but was bent or refracted out of its original direction. This was probably suggested to them by the appearance of a straight, rod partly immersed in water; and accordingly we find many questions concerning this, and other optical appearances in the works of Aristotle. It appears also from Pliny, and Lactantius, that burning glasses were known to the ancients.

Archimedes is said to have written a treatise on the appearance of a ring or circle under water, and therefore could not have been ignorant of the common phenomena of refraction.

The ancients, however, were not only acquainted with these more ordinary appearances, but also with the production of colours, by refraction. Seneca says, that if the light of the sun shines through an angular piece of glass, it will show all the colours of the rainbow. The first treatise of any consequence, on the subject of optics, was written by Ptolemy; this treatise is now lost, but from the accounts of others, we find that he treated of astronomical refractions.

The nature of refraction was afterwards considered by Alhazen, an Arabian writer; and his observations were afterwards confirmed by Vitellio, Tycho Brahe, and others.

In the writings of Roger Bacon, in the thirteenth century, we find the first distinct account of the magnifying power of glasses, and it is not improbable, that what he wrote upon this subject, gave rise to the useful invention of *Spectacles*. From this time to that of the revival of learning in Europe, we have no treatise on optics. One of the first who distinguished himself in this way, was Maurolycus, teacher of mathematics at Messina, in 1578. Baptista Porta, who died in 1515, was the inventor of the camera obscura, which throws more light on these interesting subjects. From this period, the writers on optics have been numerous and important, amongst whom Sir Isaac Newton ranks as one of the most eminent.

Glass globes, and specula, seem to have been the only optical instruments known to the ancients. Alhazen gave the first hint of the invention of spectacles. From the writings of this author, together with the observations of Roger Bacon, it is not improbable that some monks gradually hit upon the construction of spectacles. It is certain that spectacles were well known in the 13th century, and not long before. It is said, that Alexander Spina, a native of Pisa, who died in 1313, happened to see a pair of spectacles in the hands of a person who would not explain them to him, and that he succeeded in making a pair for himself, and immediately made the construction public. It is also inscribed on the tomb of Salvinus Armatus, a nobleman of Florence, who died in 1317, that he was the inventor of spectacles.

But although convex and concave lenses were sufficiently common, yet no attempt was made to combine them into a telescope, till the end of the sixteenth century. We are informed, that as James Metius was amusing himself with mirrors and burning glasses, he thought of looking through two lenses at a time: and that happening to take one that was convex, and another that was concave and happening also to hit upon a pretty good adjustment of them, he found that by looking through them, distant objects appeared very large and distinct. In fact, without knowing it, he had made a *Telescope*.

But the honour of having exhibited this arrangement of glasses in a tube, appears to Jansen, a spectacle maker, of Middleburgh in 1590. Jansen, directing his telescope to celestial objects, distinctly viewed spots on the surface of the moon, and discovered many new stars.

Galileo having made many improvements in the telescope has by some been considered as the inventor, but he himself acknowledges that he first heard of the instrument from a German. The first telescope which Gaileo constructed, magnified only three times; but soon after he made another, which magnified eighteen times; and afterwards, with great trouble and expense, he constructed one which magnified thirty three times, and with this he discovered the satellites of Jupiter, and the spots on the sun.

The honour of explaining the principles of the telescope is due to Kepler.

The principal effects of telescopes depend upon these simple principles, viz. that objects appear larger in proportion to the angles which they subtend at the eye; and that the effect is the same whether the pencils of rays by which objects are visible to us, come directly from the objects themselves, or from any place nearer to the eye where they may have been conveyed, so as to form an image of the object; because they issue again from those points when there is no real substance in certain directions, in the same manner as they did from the corresponding points in the objects themselves.

In fact, therefore, all that is effected by a telescope, is first to make such an image of a distant object by means of a lens or mirror; and then to give to the eye some assistance for viewing that image as near as possible: so that the angle which it shall subtend at the eye, may be very large compared with the angle which the object itself would subtend in the same situation. This is done by means of any eye-glass which so refracts the pencil of rays, that they may afterwards be brought to their several foci by the humours of the eye. But if the eye was so formed as to be able to see the image with sufficient distinctness at the same distance without an eye-glass, it would appear to him as much magnified as it does to another person who makes use of a glass for that purpose, though he would not in all cases have so large a field of view.

Such is the telescope which was first discovered and used by philosophers. The great inconvenience attending it is, that the field of view is exceedingly small. This inconvenience increases with the magnifying power of the telescope, so that it is a matter of surprise how, with such an instrument, Galileo and others could have made such discoveries. No other telescope, however, than this, was so much as thought of for many years after the discovery.

It is to the celebrated Kepler, that we are indebted for what we now call the astronomical telescope. The principles of this instrument are explained, and the advantages of it are clearly pointed out by this philosopher in his Catoptrics; but what is very surprising, he never actually reduced his theory to practice.

The first person who made an instrument of Kepler's construction was Scheiner, who has given a description of it in his Rosa Ursina, published in 1630. If, says he, you insert two similar lenses in a tube, and place your eye at a convenient distance, you will see all terrestrial objects inverted, indeed, but magnified and very distinct, with a considerable extent of view. He afterwards subjoins an account of a telescope of a different construction with two convex eye-glasses, which again reverses the images, and makes them appear in their natural position. This construction, however, answered the end very imperfectly, and Rheits soon after discovered a better construction, using three eye-glasses instead of two.

But these improvements and many others since made, have diminished in value by the discovery of the *reflecting* telescope; for a refracting telescope even of 1,000 feet focus, supposing it possible to be made use of, could not be made to magnify with distinctness more than 1,000 times, whereas, a reflecting telescope not exceeding nine or ten feet, will magnify 1200 times.

Mr. James Gregory of Aberdeen, was the first inventor of the reflecting telescope, but his construction is quite different from Sir Isaac Newton's, and not nearly so advantageous.

But in constructing reflecting telescopes of extraordinary magnifying powers, Sir William Herschel has displayed skill and ingenuity surpassing all his predecessors in this department of mechanics. He has made them from 7, 10, 20, to even 40 feet in length, and with instruments of these dimensions he is now employed in making discoveries in astronomy. To describe these instruments would far exceed the limits to which we are confined; but we may mention that the concave face of the metallic mirror of Sir William's largest telescope, which is fixed at the bottom of a forty-feet tube of iron, is forty-eight inches of polished surface in diameter. The thickness, which is equal in every part of it, is about three inches and a half, and its weight, when it came from the cast, was 2,118 pounds, of which it must have lost a small quantity in the polishing. The metal is an amalgam supposed to be composed of 32 parts of copper, 15 of tin. 1 of brass, 1 of silver, and 1 of arsenic: for Sir W. Herschel has not made the composition public; but Mr. Edwards, an intimate friend of his, after repeated trials, found this proportion the best for receiving a fine polish, and producing the most perfect reflection.

This instrument, with proper eye-glasses magnifies above 6,000 times, and is the largest which has ever been made.

The *achromatic* telescope was the invention of Mr. Peter Dollond.

The *micrometer* is an instrument which used with a telescope for the purpose of measuring small angles, and by the help of which the apparent magnitudes of objects viewed through a telescope or microscope, are measured with great correctness.

The *microscope* is composed of lenses or mirrors, by means of which small objects are made to appear larger that they really are to the naked eye. Microscopes are distinguished into simple, compound, and double. Simple microscopes consist of a single lens or spherule. The compound microscope consists of several lenses, duly combined. As optics have been improved, other varieties have been contrived in this instrument: hence, we have reflecting microscopes, water microscopes, botanical microscopes, solar microscopes, &c.

The *kaleidoscope* is an instrument which has lately obtained great celebrity on account of the very amusing and new forms which, by turning it round, it constantly presents to the eye. Dr. Brewster of Edinburgh has obtained a patent for the invention, an account of which may be seen in the Monthly Magazine for January, 1818. It is asserted, however, that the discovery is not a new one. For that a person named Bradley, a gardener at Hampton Court, mentions such an instrument in a work published by him more than one hundred years ago.

The mode in which the kaleidoscope is made is very simple: take a hollow tube of any dimensions, and of any length, two inches in diameter and twelve long is a convenient size: take two pieces of plate glass about one inch and a half in diameter, and one line in thickness, of a length somewhat shorter than the tube itself, and let them be fixed so that one edge may touch the other, and so as to form an angle with each other of 22 degrees; a few bits of cork may be so notched as to keep the pieces of glass in their places: the glasses are to be darkened by black painting, or some other convenient method on the exterior sides. At one end of the tube provide two circular pieces of plain clear glass, exactly the diameter of the tube into which they are to be fitted. Place between these two glasses a quantity of broken pieces of different coloured glass, the more intense and various the colours the more brilliant will the forms be, and let the pieces of broken glass be so placed as to move freely as the tube is turned round. At the opposite end of the tube let there be a small hole for the sight: the instrument will be complete; a succession of beautiful forms will then be visible, which, till experienced, would be believed absolutely impossible to be produced by any act or contrivance of man. The uses to which this instrument may be put, both useful and ornamental, it would not be easy to enumerate: it can never cease to be a constant source of amusement and delight.

Telescopes are made of various dimensions, and at a great variety of prices.

Spectacles are also an article, as is well known, in considerable request. They are made to suit eyes of different ages and of different capacities of vision. Their prices are various, depending principally upon the style in which they are mounted.

From what has been said, it is evident that an Optician should be conversant with mathematics and mechanics, and many other branches of science with which optics are connected. He should also know the history of what has been hitherto done in this art, as well as what is now doing, in order to be able to apply himself to the construction of the various instruments which it is his business to make.

The plate represents the Optician's shop, in which are seen the telescope, the microscope, spectacles, opera-glasses, &c.

THE PEWTERER

The Pewterer is a person who makes plates, dishes, pots, syringes, funnels, worms for stills, and a variety of other articles of pewter.

The trade of a Pewterer is very ancient, and although little mention is made of it in books of history, there is no doubt, from the economy of its materials for culinary purposes that it must have existed in this kingdom for many centuries.

We find in the reigns of Henry the Seventh and Eighth, that many statutes were enacted relative to the Pewterer: by 19 of the former king, cap. 6, and 4 of the same, cap. 4, the weights and standard of Pewterers' metal were limited. We find also by other statutes of Hen. VIII. that their goods were liable to be searched and sold in open places; and by the 25 of Hen. VIII. c. 9, s. 3, no stranger born shall work pewter, &c. all which proves, that in Henry the Eighth's time, the Pewterer must have been a trade of considerable importance: indeed, we apprehend much more so than at the present day, for pewter, in domestic use, except the article of pots for porter, is by no means so common as it was forty years ago. Earthenware having in a great degree superseded it.

Pewter is a factitious metal, and very uncertain in its composition. It is generally kept of different standards: that which is called plate-metal, is said to be formed of tin and regulus of antimony, in the proportions of 112 pounds of the former, to six or seven pounds of the latter.

The next inferior to this is called trifling metal, and is lowered by alloying it with lead: of this metal ale-house pots are made. Lead may be mixed with tin in any proportion, without destroying its malleability. Hence, lead and tin, with or without other smaller additions, form the pewter of ordinary use. Lead being the cheapest of the two metals, the manufacturer finds it his interest to employ it in as large a proportion as possible. But as lead is well known to be a very noxious metal, experiments have been made to ascertain in what proportion it may be mixed, with tin, without injury to the liquors for which pewter is commonly used. It has been found, when wine or vinegar was allowed to stand in vessels composed of an alloy of tin and lead, that the tin is first dissolved, whilst the lead is not acted upon by the liquors, except at the line of contact of the air and liquor; and that no sensible quantity of lead is dissolved, even by vinegar, after standing for some days in vessels that contained no more than eighteen pounds in the hundred of lead. Hence it was concluded, that as no noxious effect is produced by the very minute quantity of tin which is dissolved, pewter may be considered as perfectly safe, which contains about 80 or 82 per cent. of tin. And when vessels are employed for measure, a much less proportion of tin may be used. But it has been found that the common pewter at Paris contains no more than about 25, or 30 per cent. of tin, the remainder is lead; and there is great reason for believing that the pewter commonly used in England is of no better quality. It is evident, therefore, that the use of pewter vessels, unless the proportion of its alloy could be ascertained, is by no means desirable.

The pewterer must have an iron pot to melt the metal, a ladle to take it out; and suitable moulds for making the various articles which he manufactures: he must also have a turning lathe, for the purpose of finishing these articles which require to be rounded and true.

Pewterers have two sorts of moulds, which are commonly made of copper: those which they use for flat pewter, as dishes, plates, &c. and those which they use for hollow vessels, such as pots, &c. &c.

The moulds for flat pewter are composed of two pieces, one of which forms the upper, the other the under part of the article. These two pieces are so far apart as to permit the metal to be run, when melted, between them, to the exact shape and thickness of the article wanted.

The moulds for pots, &c. are composed of four pieces, two for the bottom, and two for the sides. Before the moulds are used, it is necessary to rub them with fine coal dust, mixed with the white of an egg, and laid in with a brush: they are afterwards to be heated.

The propriety of casting consists in the knowledge of the due degree of heat, not only of the melted metal, but also of the moulds; and this is acquired principally by experience. The finer the pewter, the hotter in general should the metal be when it is cast.

As soon as the mould is sufficiently hot, it is to be laid hold of with bits of hat, and the pieces are laid horizontally one upon the other; they are then fixed firmly together by an iron ring prepared for the purpose: it is afterwards placed on edge in such a way, that the hole of the mould having a funnel shape to it, may be easily come at. The pewter is then taken from the melting with an iron ladle, which will contain a sufficient quantity of it to make the article at once, without a second dipping. As soon as the article is cast, the mould is laid down, and the sides struck with a wooden mallet. The mould is now to be opened, and the article is taken away on the blade of a knife. And in this way the workman proceeds till he has obtained as many of the kind as are wanted.

There are many statutes relating to the manufacture and sale of pewter: one clause in the 19 Hen. 7. c. 6, we think it necessary to quote.

"No person shall make any hollow wares of pewter, to wit, salts and pots made of pewter called lay-metal, but the assize of pewter and lay-metal within London; and the maker shall mark them with their own mark, that they may avow the same by them wrought; and the same, not sufficiently made and wrought, and not marked, found in the possession of the maker or seller, shall be forfeited; and if the same be sold, the maker shall forfeit the value thereof, half to the king, and half to the finder or searcher."

The plate represents the pewterer in the act of casting some article on a bench, with dishes, syringes, &c. around him: the pot in which is the melted metal, is on the ground by his side.

THE TANNER

The art of the Tanner, consists in converting the gelatinous part of the skins of animals, into the substance called leather, by impregnating it with tannin, or the tanning principle, in such a way as to render it tenacious, durable, and impenetrable to water.

It is difficult to say at what period the art of tanning was discovered. It was doubtless known to the ancients in some degree of perfection; and it is highly probably that the skins of animals were employed by man as a covering, long before the art of tanning was known: but they would require, in this state, to be constantly kept dry, as moisture would soon bring them into a state of putrefaction.

The astringent matter which converts the skin into leather, abounds in so many vegetables in every country, that accident would soon lead to some method of producing the change. Independent, however, of vegetables, many earthy and metallic substances have the property of rendering skins incorruptible to a certain extent; and some mineral waters, containing copper or iron, will occasion this change. Hence we may conclude that some means of giving preference to the skins, must have been known at a very early period.

Though there has been no radical alteration, or any great practical improvements in the art of tanning, yet for the last twenty or thirty years, it has attracted the attention of many celebrated chemists and philosophers in all countries, who have investigated the subject with great accuracy and precision. Previous to this period we occasionally find some experiments and observations by men of science on the materials of tanning. A variety of patents has also been obtained in this country for improvements in the art of tanning, but we cannot speak of them as having effectuated much important advantage to the art. The last patent is one which promises, according to the specification, to shorten the time, and improve the process of tanning; and if the assertions of the patentee, W.A. Ronalds, of Hammersmith, be correct, leather, by his process, can be tanned in a few weeks. An account of this patent may be seen in the Monthly Magazine for July, 1818.

All tanned leather is classed and universally known under two general denominations: namely, *hides* and *skins*. The former being commonly applied to the larger animals, as bulls, oxen, cows, &c. whose skins are chiefly intended for the soles of stout shoes, and other purposes, requiring very thick and solid leather; while the latter term is used for calves' seals' skins, &c. which being thinner and more flexible, are intended for the upper leather of shoes and boots, for saddles, harness, &c.

The stoutest and heaviest of the bull and ox hides, are generally selected to make what are technically called *butts* or backs, and are manufactured in the following manner:

When the horns, &c. have been removed, the raw hides are laid in a heap for two or three days, and are then suspended on poles in a close room, called a smoke-house, which is heated somewhat above the common temperature by a mouldering fire: this occasions incipient putrefaction, which loosens the epidermis, and renders the hair, and other extraneous matter, easy of separation from the true skin. This is effected by extending the hide on a wooden horse or beam of a convex form, and scraping it with a large two-handled knife, called a *fleshing-knife*, which is bent to suit the convexity of the beam. The hides are then immersed in a pit, containing water slightly impregnated with sulphuric acid. This operation, which is called *raising*, by distending the pores and swelling the fibres, prepares the hide for the reception of the tanner, and renders it more susceptible of its action.

When the hides are sufficiently *raised*, they are removed into a pit, in which they are laid smooth with a layer of oak bark, ground to a coarse powder, between each.

The pit is then filled with the tanning lixivium, or ooze, prepared from oak bark and water, and the hides remain a month or six weeks without being moved. At the end of this time the tanning principle being exhausted, the ooze and spent bark are taken out of the pit, and the hides put in again in the same way with fresh bark, and covered with fresh ooze as before. Here they remain about three months, when the same process is repeated at about the same intervals, three several times or more, according to the strength of the lixivium, and the substance of the hides. When sufficiently tanned, they are taken out of the pit, hung up in a shed to dry gradually, and being compressed with a steel instrument, and beaten smooth to render them fine and dense, the operation is complete; and, having been numbered, and weighed and stamped by the excise officer, they are ready for sale, and are termed *butts* or backs.

Crop hides are thus manufactured. The horns having been removed, the hides are immersed in pits, containing a mixture of lime and water, where they remain three or four days, being occasionally moved up and down that every part may be uniformly exposed to the action of the lime-water. They are then taken out of the lime-pits, and the hair and other extraneous matter being scraped off, on a wooden beam as before described, are washed in water to free them from the lime and filth adhering. They are now immersed in a weak ooze, and by degrees are removed into other pits containing solutions, gradually increasing in strength during the time that they are taken up and put down, (technically termed *handling*,) at least once in every day, that all the parts of the hide may be acted upon by the tanning principle equally and uniformly. This is continued for about a month or six weeks, when they are put into other pits with stronger ooze, and a small portion of ground bark; whence, as the tannin becomes exhausted, they are removed to other pits in regular succession, with fresh ooze and fresh bark for two or three months.

At the end of this period, the hides are put into larger vats called *layers*, in which they are laid smooth in a lixivium of greater strength, and with a larger quantity of ground bark between each fold. Here they remain about six weeks, when they are taken up and relaid in the same manner, with fresh bark and strong ooze for two months. This process is repeated with little variation once, twice, or thrice, at the discretion of the manufacturer, till the hides are thoroughly tanned; when they are taken out of the pits, suspended on poles to dry, and being compressed and smoothed nearly in the same manner as before described, are called *crop hides*, and form the principal sole leather of England.

The process of tanning calves' and seals' skins, &c. is somewhat different. They are continued in the lime pits for ten or fifteen days; they are then deprived of their hair, and washed in water, after which they are immersed in an infusion of pigeons' dung, called a *grainer*, having the property of an alkali. In this they remain for a week or ten days, according to the state of the atmosphere, and other circumstances, during which time they are frequently handled and scraped on both sides upon a convex wooden beam. This scraping, or working as it is termed, with the action of the *grainer*, helps to discharge all the lime, oil, and saponaceous matter, and renders the skins soft and plaint, and fitted to imbibe the tanning principle. They are now removed into pits containing a weak solution of bark, where they undergo nearly the same process of handling, &c. as *crop hide*; but they are seldom placed in layers: and the time occupied in tanning them is usually from two to four months, according to their nature and substance. The skins are then dried, and sold to the currier, who dresses and blacks them for the upper leathers of boots, shoes, for harness, and various other purposes.

The light and thin sort of cow-hides and horse-hides, undergo nearly the same process in tanning as calves' skins, and are applied to similar uses.

Tanned leather is subject to a heavy excise duty, amounting to *three pence* per pound.

Tanners are obliged to take out an annual license from the board of excise, and are besides subject to a variety of fiscal regulations and penalties, which, for the honour of a free state, and the advantages of trade, it would be well if they did not exist.

The trade of a tanner cannot be carried on without considerable capital; and a roomy yard, sheds, and pits, with plenty of water, are indispensable requisites.

The plate represents a tan-yard, as it is usually seen in the neighbourhood of the metropolis.

CONTENTS OF VOLUME I

CONTENTS OF VOLUME II